Eating
DISORDERS

Eating
DISORDERS
A Question and Answer Book About Anorexia Nervosa and Bulimia Nervosa

Ellen Erlanger

Lerner Publications Company
Minneapolis

The essays in chapter five are reprinted from the *NAAS Newsletter* by the kind permission of the authors.

The illustrations in this book are reproduced from *Women: A Pictorial Archive from Nineteenth-Century Sources* by Jim Harter, copyright © 1978 by Dover Publications, Inc., and *Humorous Victorian Spot Illustrations* by Carol Belanger Grafton, copyright © 1985 by Dover Publications, Inc.

Resource list on pages 56-61 courtesy of National Anorexic Aid Society.

LIBRARY OF CONGRESS CATALOGING-IN-PUBLICATION DATA

Erlanger, Ellen.
  Eating disorders: a question and answer book about anorexia nervosa and bulimia nervosa / Ellen Erlanger.
      p.   cm.
  Bibliography: p.
  Includes index.
  Summary: Questions and answers present information about the emotional and psychological motivations, warning signs, symptoms, and dangers of anorexia and bulimia. Includes first-person accounts by women who have suffered from these eating disorders.
  ISBN 0-8225-0038-8 (lib. bdg.)
  1. Anorexia nervosa — Miscellanea — Juvenile literature.
2. Bulimia — Miscellanea — Juvenile literature. [1. Anorexia nervosa. 2. Bulimia. 3. Questions and answers.] I. Title.
RC552.A5E75   1988
616.85'2 — dc19   87-15311
                                                                   CIP
                                                                   AC

Manufactured in the United States of America

  2 3 4 5 6 7 8 9 10 98 97 96 95 94 93 92 91 90 89 88

Contents

Introduction

Without even realizing it, you probably know someone who has an eating disorder. Millions of people have suffered from severe problems related to their patterns of eating or dieting—problems known as *anorexia nervosa* and *bulimia nervosa*.

An eating disorder is not a sign of weakness or foolishness in a person. An eating disorder can happen to anyone. Many famous people—including stars like Jane Fonda, Cathy Rigby, Susan Dey, and Ally Sheedy—have struggled with these problems.

Perhaps someone close to you is struggling, too. It's time to find out more about why.

CHAPTER ONE

What Happened to Dana

Dana's diet started in a normal way. She wanted to lose a few pounds so she'd look better in her bathing suit. Many of her friends dieted that summer, too.

But by mid-fall there was a disturbing difference between Dana and her eighth-grade companions. She was the only one who had never stopped trying to lose weight. In fact, she was trying harder than ever—even though she was already down to a weak-looking eighty pounds.

At lunchtime the year before, Dana had usually eaten pizza or a sandwich and potato chips, a piece of fruit, and dessert. Now she ate nothing at all. She brought a can of diet soda and sipped it for half an hour while her friends ate.

Though she ate very little, Dana still seemed full of energy. In gym class she worked harder than anyone else, often putting in extra exercise time. To her this was a way of burning a few more calories. She drove herself to the limit.

The gym teacher was pleased with Dana's effort but worried about her health. She called her aside one day after class.

"Dana, I'm concerned about you," she began slowly. "You've lost so much weight since last spring. Are you feeling all right?"

"Sure, I feel great," Dana answered. "I can move a lot better without all that excess weight."

"Well, just be careful that you don't lose *too* much weight, Dana. Some girls let their diets get out of hand, you know. You're already beginning to look a little ghostly."

"I'm fine, Mrs. Tate, honestly. There's no problem."

Dana didn't see the problem then, but she *was* letting her diet get out of hand. Thinness had become her major goal. She couldn't think about eating without feeling guilty. She *had* to control her calorie count. When others urged her to eat, she became even more determined to diet. She had to keep proving her willpower.

Meanwhile, she was not dealing well with other pressures in her life. She couldn't seem to understand her French class this year, and she knew her grades were going to go down. Two of her friends had boyfriends now, and whenever she saw them they kept asking which boy she was interested in. She didn't know what to say to them. She was kind of scared to think about dating someone. And to top it off, her brother and sister couldn't seem to talk to each other without getting into a fight. Sometimes

she just went into her room and shut the door, but she could still hear them yelling at each other. Her parents tried to keep the peace, but they didn't get home until 6:30 most nights, and that left plenty of time for arguments. The only part of her life that she felt like she controlled was her diet. No matter what anyone said or did, Dana was still in charge of what she put in her body.

Without knowing it, Dana was suffering from an eating disorder called *anorexia nervosa*. Sometimes people call it anorexia for short, or just "the dieting disease." It involves self-starving and many other complications. Unfortunately, it is becoming a more common problem. Experts estimate that at least 1 in every 200 females between the ages of 12 and 18 suffers from anorexia nervosa, and that the percentage is significantly higher among wealthier families. It is apparently occurring more frequently among males as well.

Another eating disorder, *bulimia nervosa*, is far more common. This disorder, more commonly known as bulimia, is perhaps even epidemic in recent years. Statistics vary from one study to another, but it appears that as many as one-fourth of all college-age women may develop bulimic symptoms. And the disorder is affecting growing numbers of both men and women above and below college age.

As you will soon learn, bulimia is not a self-starving disease, but instead a "self-stuffing" disease in which the person eats large amounts of food and then feels that he or she must get rid of it in order to avoid weight gain and remain a "worthy" individual. Obviously, in both disorders, the individual's eating patterns are out of control.

Those who suffer from anorexia are known as *anorexics,* or less commonly as anorectics. Those who have bulimia are called *bulimics.* Sometimes people go back and forth between anorexic and bulimic patterns. Or they may have certain anorexic or bulimic symptoms without displaying the full *syndrome,* the characteristic set of symptoms associated with a diagnosed disorder.

More than nine times out of ten, people with eating disorders are females. So the pronouns "she" and "her" are commonly used in describing their individual cases. But as we've said, that doesn't mean that males aren't affected, too.

As we've said, anorexia and bulimia affect people of many different ages. Many cases have been reported among preadolescents and middle-aged women. But the most common time for problems to start seems to be between the ages of twelve and twenty-five. The earlier an eating disorder is identified, the better the chances for recovery. Without appropriate professional help, eating disorders can continue for many years. So it is important for students, their parents, and their teachers to know more about anorexia and bulimia.

These disorders are not easy to understand. Studying anorexia and bulimia requires considerable effort and information. Here are a few reasons why:

- Anorexia and bulimia affect a person's thoughts and feelings as well as his or her body. So we say that they are *psychological and emotional disorders as well as physical ones.* This makes them much more complicated than illnesses like measles or mononucleosis, also known as "mono."
- Most anorexics and bulimics are people who seem to "have everything going for them." They are usually high achievers from families with good incomes. It is hard to imagine why they have such problems.
- Although anorexics and bulimics share certain concerns, each case is unique. There are many different ways in which someone with an eating disorder may think or behave. So we need to consider individual characteristics as well as more common ones.
- There is still a great deal that we *don't* know about anorexia and bulimia. Until recently there was very little research about eating disorders. Many doctors, nurses, and mental health professionals are just beginning to study and treat them.

This book will help you examine both general ideas and individual cases related to anorexia and bulimia. It is meant to provide a basic introduction to these disorders, not a complete analysis. But several sources of further information are supplied at the end. So if you still have questions after you've read this book— and you probably will—feel free to consult the sources listed.

In the meantime, let's begin by responding to some of the questions most frequently asked about eating disorders.

CHAPTER TWO

Signs and Symptoms

The first thing to know about eating disorders is how to identify them. Bulimics and anorexics often have characteristic patterns of behavior. If you know the characteristics of the disorder and can spot the warning signs, you have taken the first step toward getting help for someone with the disorder.

These are the first questions people commonly ask about eating disorders.

What do we mean by an "eating disorder"?

An eating disorder is a severe disturbance of a person's eating habits. The person's behavior in regard to food and eating becomes markedly different from normal behavior. We can see that a disturbance or abnormal pattern exists because:

- The person's way of either eating or not eating is out of control.
- Other people are affected in a negative way by the person's change of habits and behavior.
- The person is usually preoccupied with food—either pursuing it or avoiding it.
- The person is unhappy—nervous, depressed, guilty, and/or lonely.
- The person's eating or dieting pattern interferes with his or her relationships and responsibilities.
- The person's health is in danger.

What are the major characteristics of anorexia nervosa?

Anorexia nervosa is characterized by an extreme and intense fear of gaining weight, which leads the person to pursue continuous weight loss. To an anorexic, "the thinner the better." Sometimes a diet can begin innocently, like Dana's. But anorexics don't stop dieting at a reasonable point. They keep going until their lives may even be threatened. When doctors are trying to determine whether someone is anorexic or not, they usually look for a significant weight loss, plus other characteristics of an anorexic pattern.

Anorexics may use other methods of weight loss along with dieting or fasting. They may use excessive exercise, diet pills, laxatives (medications to stimulate bowel movements), diuretics (also known as water pills because they stimulate urination), or vomiting as ways of feeling thinner or controlling calories. But whatever the method, the primary goal is thinness.

You may wonder why anorexics don't stop dieting once they become skinny. The reason is that a major characteristic of anorexia is a problem called *distorted body image.* This means that anorexics view their

bodies very differently than other people do. When they look in the mirror, they never see themselves as being too thin. They "feel fat" and tend to overestimate their weight. If an anorexic is told she is too skinny, she is more likely to be happy than upset. She may not like being bugged about her weight—but she is glad people are noticing her "new body." She probably does not believe she has a problem.

But she does. She is using weight reduction as an unhealthy way of coping with other pressures. She may not even realize what these areas of stress are until she begins treatment for her disorder—but somewhere inside her they exist. These emotional or "nervous" reasons for the disturbed eating pattern explain why the word "nervosa" is part of the disorder's complete name.

The word "anorexia" means "lack of appetite." But that doesn't necessarily mean anorexics aren't hungry. Generally they *do* crave food, but they deny their feelings. Deep down, most of them long to eat—so much that they may dream about food or become focused on cooking for others. But despite their very real hunger, their struggle for thinness is more important to them.

What are the warning signs of anorexia nervosa?

Look for the following:
- significant, abnormal weight loss with no known medical cause
- reduction of food intake, especially of high-calorie items
- denial of hunger, including claims of "feeling full" or "feeling fat" after just a few bites
- excessive exercise in spite of fatigue
- extreme fear of weight gain
- strange patterns of handling food, e.g., pushing it around on the plate but not eating it, developing "food rituals"
- strong interest in cooking and/or reading about

food, but refusal to enjoy it in the company of others
- disruption or halt of menstruation
- changes in personality and behavior—especially if those changes include increased withdrawal, irritability, nervousness, and depression

What are the major characteristics of bulimia nervosa?

Translated from its Greek roots, the word *bulimia* means "ox hunger" or "animal hunger." Bulimia is characterized by *binge eating* (uncontrollable overeating) followed by *purging*, most commonly in the form of forced vomiting or abuse of laxatives. Bulimics consume large quantities (sometimes up to ten thousand calories—in extreme cases, more) of food during binges, and much of the food is high in carbohydrates and fats. Bulimics usually binge in secret and are ashamed of their behavior afterwards.

Much of their motivation for purging comes from a need to "cleanse" and empty the body after a binge to restore a sense of well-being.

Bulimics commonly try to stop the binge-purge cycle by fasting or dieting strictly and exercising instead. But it is very difficult for them to give up their pattern of overeating and then vomiting or using large amounts of laxatives and/or diuretics. Their binge-purge cycle often serves as an outlet for painful feelings like anger, frustration, boredom, loneliness, and disappointment. Bulimics seem to lack healthier ways of expressing their feelings.

Bulimics share some characteristics with anorexics. Both are extremely preoccupied with food and weight control, and both use extreme methods to pursue this control. Both use weight control as a substitute for dealing with other issues and pressures. Both may tend to be *perfectionists*—focused on being the best at everything, including at achieving the "perfect weight," however they may define it.

But bulimics are different from anorexics in many ways. While anorexics turn *away from* food to cope, bulimics turn *to* food. While anorexics deny their problem, bulimics generally recognize that their patterns are abnormal. They are usually trying to maintain their weight rather than lose more and more, and their perceptions of their bodies are not as distorted as the body images of anorexics. However, they are more likely than anorexics to have accompanying problems such as alcohol abuse or shoplifting.

Though bulimics far outnumber anorexics, it is much harder to identify them. Whereas anorexics appear emaciated from extreme weight loss, bulimics are usually within ten to fifteen pounds of normal body weight. They are secretive about their binging yet are more outgoing on the surface than anorexics. Though they know they need help, they usually suffer in silence and shame for a long time before seeking assistance.

What are the warning signs of bulimia nervosa?

Look for the following:
- any evidence of a binge-purge cycle
- concern about weight and attempts to control it through dieting, vomiting, or laxative and diuretic abuse
- eating pattern which may alternate between binges and fasts
- concern for secrecy
- frequent use of bathroom for vomiting or diarrhea
- consumption of high-calorie food during binges (although the food may be consumed in secret, you might find evidence of it, such as empty containers in the trash)
- fairly normal body weight, but strong concern for weight maintenance
- depressive moods and self-punishing thoughts after binges

CHAPTER THREE

Causes and Cautions

Now that you know a little more about eating disorders—what they are and how to recognize them—you need to know about the causes and dangers of bulimia and anorexia. You can be much more persuasive in getting help if you understand why someone might suffer from the disorder and just how dangerous it can be to the person's health. The questions and answers in this chapter explain these subjects.

What emotional issues or pressures contribute to anorexia and bulimia?

Each case is different—and the anorexic or bulimic is often not aware of what is bothering her until she begins treatment for her disorder. Even if she does recognize sources of stress in her life, she may not consciously connect them with her eating pattern.

Though both anorexia and bulimia are very individual problems, certain issues or stress factors seem to occur more commonly than others. Some difficulties that are reported frequently are:

- Relationships or conditions in the person's life change suddenly. There may be a death or divorce in the family, a change in friends, a romantic breakup, or a new job, place of residence, or school.
- The person may fear or experience failure in some important activity. Although she is usually a high achiever, she may be afraid she cannot continue to excel. Common sources of pressure are school, sports, or work.
- If she's a preteen or teenager, the person may be insecure about her new physical appearance and feelings of sexuality. Anorexics in particular may cling to the "shelter of childhood." Thinness de-emphasizes the hips and breasts and may cause menstruation to stop, thus returning the anorexic to "childhood."
- The person may be trying to break out of her dependence on others. If she has been strongly protected or overshadowed, she may be seeking some way to fight back or take a stand. She does not feel comfortable asserting herself in more normal ways.

- On the other hand, the person may feel that she has not been protected and guided enough by her family, that she has been abandoned. This may lead to anger and resentment, and an eating disorder may be her way of hiding these feelings.
- The person may be involved in an activity with a strong focus on weight control and may thus have trouble keeping weight issues in perspective. Dancers, wrestlers, gymnasts, models, actors, jockeys, cheerleaders, distance runners, and others whose bodies are constantly on display are at greater risk. Of course, other factors help determine whether eating disorders develop or not. But people whose activities provide a built-in preoccupation with weight need to be especially cautious.
- The person may attach her basic drives for perfection to our culture's emphasis on thinness. Some people can "stay skinny" but still keep their dieting under control and within reason. Others—those who are insecure and perfectionistic, who have trouble saying, "I'm OK the way I am"—find this much harder.

causes — ## How has our culture contributed to eating disorders?

We live in a culture which places great emphasis on outward appearances. We are very weight-conscious, and the value we place on thinness has grown in recent decades. We admire people who are trim, and we look down upon people who are overweight. For example, the average weight of Miss America Pageant contestants and winners has gone down every year for the last twenty years. And since 1970, the winners have weighed significantly less than the other contestants.

These attitudes are established at a very early age in America. Preschoolers who are given a choice of thin dolls or chubby ones tend to choose the thin ones. By the second grade, youngsters describe overweight classmates as "lazy" and "stupid," even though these labels are inaccurate and unfair. When children become teenagers, the message they see and hear in the media is clear: "Thin is in!"

So dieting is a natural part of American life. Most of us are concerned about our weight, and most of us try to control it from time to time. But for some people, weight control and patterns of food use get out of hand. And this is probably more likely to occur in a culture with values like ours—where consumption is encouraged but thinness is praised more highly.

causes

What do we know about physical causes of eating disorders?

Several researchers are studying physical causes, but they have not yet reached any definite conclusions. Some experts suspect that problems with the hypothalamus gland or other parts of the body's hormone system may increase a person's chances of having an eating disorder. But these experts still emphasize the importance of emotional factors in promoting these problems. When a person who has emotional "risk factors" tries dieting, the dieting itself can lead to changes in the way the person thinks, feels, and behaves.

effects

Blairsville Junior High School
Blairsville, Pennsylvania

What physical dangers can result from eating disorders?

The hazards are numerous, and they fall into several categories. First, there are the effects of extreme weight loss: slower heart rate and reflexes, increased sensitivity to cold, weakness, tendency toward mild anemia, and susceptibility to infection. Skin, hair, and nails become dry and brittle. Fine, downy hair called *lanugo* may grow in new places to conserve body heat. Most females stop menstruating, though emotional or hormonal factors may contribute to this, too, since a significant number stop menstruating before weight loss begins.

Beyond the effects of weight loss itself, there may be side effects from the weight reduction methods used. Vomiting, laxatives, and diuretics all disturb the balance of potassium and sodium in the body. When this balance is disrupted, the anorexic or bulimic may experience results ranging from heart irregularities and kidney problems to dizziness, fatigue, depression, and irritability.

Particularly dangerous are drugs used to cause vomiting. Singer Karen Carpenter is thought to have died from heart problems resulting from her long battle with anorexia, and the medication she used to induce vomiting may have played a role.

Binge eating and purging may cause many other problems. From the stress of excessive eating and vomiting and the stomach acids that accompany the vomit, the bulimic may develop a puffy mouth and jaw, a persistent sore throat, inflamed esophagus, dental problems, abdominal pain, and other complications.

Eating disorders *can* be life-threatening. Somewhere between five and fifteen percent of anorexics die from their illness. The rate is not as high for bulimics, but years of struggle with the binge-purge cycle can cause severe problems for the individuals involved. And deaths can occur from bulimia, particularly as a result of heart failure, kidney failure, and suicide.

What emotional dangers can result?

An eating disorder is a lonely and confusing experience. Anorexics and bulimics can feel isolated, rejected, and defeated. The eating disorder is triggered by emotional problems, and in turn it triggers new stresses and concerns. Anorexics or bulimics have to face these new issues and conflicts that result from their disorders, and it is painful to deal with new concerns on top of their old ones. The result is extreme stress and a genuine need for help.

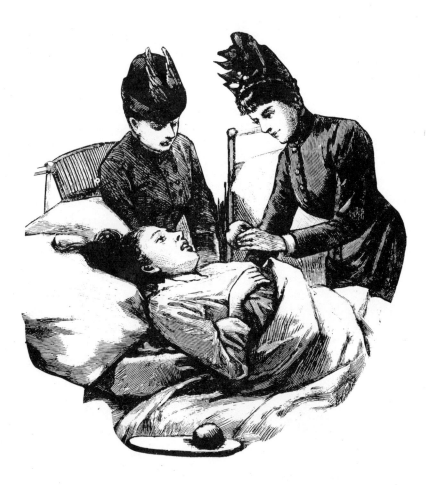

CHAPTER FOUR

Help and Hope

Now that you can recognize an eating disorder and know something about its causes, you are ready to find out how it can be treated. People do recover from eating disorders, but they need help to make it. The questions and answers in this chapter explain what kinds of help are available and what to do for a friend who resists getting help.

What kinds of help are recommended for those with eating disorders?

A combination of medical and psychological help is usually recommended. Of course, the amount and nature of the help depends on the extent of the problem. In cases where medical and counseling professionals feel that a person's life and/or stability is in danger, *hospitalization* is necessary. The top priority is keeping the person alive. Counseling can begin once physical strength is restored.

Counseling therapy is also recommended in non-hospital cases and may take a number of forms. *One-to-one sessions* generally provide the foundation for treatment. At first the therapist and client usually talk about concerns regarding weight, food, and body image and set goals for establishing more normal patterns. In later stages of therapy the individual should be working on relationship issues, self-esteem, and positive ways of coping with stress. As these underlying emotional factors are addressed, the chances of recovery are greatly increased.

If *group therapy* is used, a therapist works with a number of persons with eating disorders, more commonly bulimics. Members of the group can share their experiences and feelings, draw upon each other for strength, and therefore feel less alone in their struggle. The therapist guides the group so that discussions are directed at helping each member achieve progress in recovery.

Support groups are also useful, although they serve a different function than actual therapy. Support groups offer a safe environment in which anorexics or bulimics or their families can learn more about eating disorders and share their concerns about them. Groups are sometimes led by professional counselors, but they may also be led by recovered individuals or family members of anorexics or bulimics.

Family or *couples therapy* may be used when the

therapist feels that family issues and attitudes have contributed to the disorder, or that the family's strengths can be used to help solve underlying problems. The therapist will observe the family's communication patterns, decision-making patterns, roles, and values and give recommendations for ways to improve communication. Such help can be especially helpful to adolescent clients and their families, or to couples whose relationships are *in distress* (undergoing severe strain).

Recently, there has been increased interest in the use of *antidepression drugs* in the treatment of bulimia. Continued research is needed, but the outlook from several studies appears promising. Of course, counseling is still recommended along with the drug treatment.

Nutritional counseling is another useful aid in treating eating disorders. Anorexics and bulimics often need assistance from a health care professional in deciding which foods to include in a more sensible eating pattern.

To help their clients return to more normal eating habits, some doctors or counselors use methods of *behavior modification*. These help the individual make step-by-step progress by awarding certain privileges in return for healthy behavior. Sometimes "food diaries" (written logs of what is eaten and when, including notes about quantity, circumstances, and resulting feelings) are used to help anorexics or bulimics see their own eating patterns more clearly.

Help from professionals is very valuable. But so is assistance from others who have suffered or are suffering from anorexia. *Self-help organizations* have been growing in the past several years. Groups in many cities sponsor activities and newsletters for anorexics and bulimics, their parents, and interested others. (See the list of organizations at the end of the book.)

What can I do if I know an anorexic or bulimic who is resisting help?

This question does not have an easy answer. It is painful to see someone we care about suffer and change. But as a concerned individual, there are some helpful steps you can take.

Continue to keep yourself "open" and informed. As you gather information, try to share some useful literature with the individual and offer to discuss it with her or him. Often increased awareness will motivate the person to seek assistance.

But sometimes more aggressive encouragement is needed. If you believe the person's symptoms and actions are affecting others as well as harming her or him, be honest and direct about this. But also assure the person that he or she is not alone and will be given support during treatment.

If you are a minor, share your concerns (especially about another young person) with an adult who can help. This may be someone at school (nurse, counselor, teacher, principal), a parent, a religious leader, or anyone else you trust. Encouraging a peer to seek help is a difficult task and a heavy responsibility—so find someone to support you in this effort. It may be necessary for someone to express concern to the person's parent(s), and family members may be reluctant at first to acknowledge a potential problem.

But try not to give up! People with eating disorders and their families often struggle with "denial," but the persistence of concerned others can make a significant difference in what happens.

As you can tell from the example in chapter one, that is exactly what happened in Dana's case. Although she continued to deny that she had a problem, her gym teacher and one of her friends finally got through to her family, then to her. She and her parents participated in support groups as well as counseling. Her brother and sister went to some of the sessions too. In counseling, Dana learned other ways to cope with her fears and her stresses.

Dana's family would have taken much longer to seek help if others hadn't kept urging them to do so.

Dana's recovery was much easier to achieve because people who cared about her intervened early, as soon as they noticed the problem.

Even if the individual rejects help, it is a good idea for family and friends to seek assistance. Counseling, family support groups, community awareness sessions, and other services may help to ease the hurt and tension that accompany anorexia nervosa and bulimia nervosa. And these "helping strategies" can also provide experiences that will motivate the individual to seek treatment and to change.

CHAPTER FIVE

First Person Views of Anorexia and Bulimia

trans. to case study

By now you should have a general picture of how anorexia and bulimia affect people. But the deepest impact of the illness is best described by those who have experienced it.

So prepare to meet Pat and Joan. Their stories will open up a far more personal side of eating disorders for you.

Patricia Howe Tilton, the author of the first account, deserves special recognition for her role in getting self-help for anorexics off the ground. In 1976, Helen Bottel, a King Features newspaper columnist, printed a letter from the anguished father of an anorexic. She received thousands of responses, including one from Pat, who was hoping to start a nationwide network of communication for people affected by anorexia. Pat's determination and Helen's support soon led to the founding of the National Anorexic Aid Society (NAAS) in Columbus, Ohio.

NAAS has been instrumental in helping concerned people throughout the country start their own support groups. Hundreds of these groups now exist to help anorexics, bulimics, and those who care about them.

The *NAAS Newsletter* is published several times a year and has received thousands of letters since its first printing in October 1977. The accounts you are about to read first appeared in the *NAAS Newsletter.*

Anorexia: My Search for Acceptance

by Patricia Howe Tilton

What are some of the discoveries I have been making about myself?

I am feeling alive and even liking myself. I am finding inner fulfillment. I am living my life as "me."

Sharing my own authentic experiences with anorexia nervosa—my positive and painful experiences—is the most caring thing I can do.

Before my diagnosis of anorexia nervosa and during

the early stages of my therapy, I was a very fearful, isolated, and sickly individual. I pursued a course of starvation as a means of living my daily life. My anorexia did not begin overnight, as there were signs of it in my life at twelve years of age. But my actual starvation was never really apparent until I was

twenty-three. Anorexia had become a way of life for me—an ineffective and incompetent way of handling my emotional problems. I had half-starved myself all of my life and knew no other way to live. As I grew older my problems became more numerous and I began to rely more on my "not eating" to live my life.

I never felt OK with myself during my adolescent and early adult years. I didn't know what I looked like. Vague feelings of not being normal or acceptable gnawed at me. I was so afraid I was crazy, since I didn't know anyone else who acted the way I did. I lived in secret with the fear that someone would find me out and expose me to the world. I wanted to fade away unnoticed. The pain I felt was unbearable and caused me to turn on myself. I was so ashamed of myself... hated myself... scolded myself... and promised myself many times it wouldn't happen again. But my anorexia would always reappear as a defense to protect me from the conflict I felt.

Sometimes my feelings of wanting to fade away would alternate with feelings of wanting to be accepted. I wanted to be someone. College afforded me the opportunity to create a positive identity for myself. I studied journalism. I directed all my energies toward creating "the journalist me"—an identity that was ambitious, self-assured, fearless, and successful. I only let people know the journalist me. I separated my intellect from the "emotional me." I was obsessed with trying to outdo myself professionally. I won writing awards and received job promotions, but none of these things ever fulfilled me. I was searching for something more.

My body was becoming sick because I was depriving it of feelings and of nourishment. My weight was very low and I was hardly eating. I felt no hunger.

My physician helped me discover that my illness was related to emotional stress and to my not eating. I was scared and found myself with my nose in a book trying to understand what was happening to me. I couldn't run from myself any longer. I discovered I was anorexic and I began psychotherapy.

My own world opened to me during my next few years of therapy. Therapy was a slow and trying experience. I had my setbacks, but I had to expect this as anorexia had become a way of life for me, and I couldn't expect to lick it overnight. I began to make a lot of progress when I realized that "not eating" was not my real problem—it was only a mask for the emotional problems and pain within me.

My doctors encouraged me to throw away my scales. They helped me to get to know myself. I began to discover my own thoughts and feelings, recognize my body signals of stress and anxiety, and deal with painful feelings before I would push them underground. As I found more constructive ways of dealing with my problems, I found I didn't need starvation to help me cope. My eating began to correct itself.

During the past few years I've been working hard to build my own healthy body and mind—something that is taking time, patience, and a knowledge of myself. I have been following a nutritional plan and making time for relaxation, exercise, and hobbies. I have become more caring to myself.

My life and my work have taken on new dimensions and I am growing in both areas now. Learning about myself has been a very precious and priceless opportunity for me—something I will never stop doing. It took a lot of work for me to be such an isolated and non-feeling person, but it has taken even more work for me to be myself and to share myself with others.

Food Was My Entire Life

by Joan Carson

I had a fantasy as a child—I wanted to live alone on an island, away from the rest of the world. On my island I would have no problems or responsibilities. I could be carefree, happy, at play.

Yet being alone terrified me. And I was very dependent on my family. "Growing up" frightened me, and I didn't want to become a teenager. I wanted to stay little forever.

Inside I hurt. I wanted attention and affection, but never felt like I received any. My family told me they loved me, but I never felt loved. I felt empty inside.

To fulfill this empty feeling within me, I found food. At age thirteen, food became my entire life. Food was the only thing I ever looked forward to—it was to become my entire existence during the next twelve years. I was obsessed with food and thought about it day and night.

My binging began when I was thirteen years old, shortly after I lost weight on a doctor's diet. I was very satisfied with my weight loss, but having denied myself most of the foods I really desired, I then found I really had no control over my eating. I always envied other girls my age who could eat without gaining weight. I loved eating, but was terrified of becoming fat.

Therefore I turned to what I believed to be the "miracle cure" for staying slim. I would eat as much as I wanted and then would vomit immediately. This way I could stay the same weight, but gorge myself on food.

This activity became a daily routine. It was all I ever lived for, and I practiced this ritual until only a slight touch on my throat would bring up the food. I ate everything I could get my hands on. I estimate I consumed 40,000 calories a day, but never gained a pound. I was secretive and cagey and had my ritual down to a fine art. I couldn't stop, and seeking help was useless because I always lied to both my doctors and parents.

During my college years I was very unhappy and

isolated from the world and my peers. I was living away from home and among strangers. I wanted their acceptance and was fearful that I might not be able to keep my secret. I didn't want anyone to know about the true me, so I developed a very bizarre eating pattern to cope with my addiction. For hours at a time I would eat, but discard my food before it could be swallowed. I collected paper cups so I could throw it away without being caught. No food was entering my

system, and I began to lose weight. At the end of my sophomore year I weighed ninety pounds at a height of five feet four inches.

My goal was to be as thin as possible so I could eat as much as I wanted without getting fat. Thin was acceptable, not fat.

Eight years had passed since I started binging and vomiting. I truly hated myself and the world I lived in. My body began to rebel. I lost my sense of taste. I felt a numbness around my nose. I had messed up my sinuses and I had a sore throat all the time. But I was too stubborn to give up my ways. Food was my life—it was all I had.

My relationship with my family started to become very strained after I moved home following college graduation. They knew what I was doing but didn't understand. My behavior began to take its toll on the entire household. The family wanted me to get well, but I hated them for this. I discovered that the only people I really ever cared about wouldn't have anything to do with me. I was dependent on my family but was living "alone" among them. They became cold toward me. I received icy stares and felt ignored. Feelings of rejection drove me from my home.

I was alone—alone on my own little island. I needed my family but could not go back. I was totally disgusted with what I had become and I felt I was beyond anyone's help. I retreated to my binging. During the day I would starve myself, and then I would spend my evening eating for four to five hours until I felt full inside. But then I felt guilty if I felt full, because this meant I couldn't eat again until I was empty. I wanted to eat because eating filled the emptiness I felt within me. I felt love in food.

I was on a merry-go-round and couldn't get off. Within six months I had dropped to eighty-five pounds.

I wanted to lose more weight because I felt fat. I knew everyone could see the hamburger, french fries, and cake in my stomach. I hated the weight in my stomach. I continued to lose.

Then on Christmas day I came down with the flu. I was very ill, and my family found me nearly dead at eighty pounds. They took me home. They *did* care. I

had been wanting them to say, "Joan, come home," for a very long time. My recovery was a very slow and long struggle. I was seriously ill and frightened. After twelve years of binging and vomiting I knew I had to stop before I killed myself. I went "cold turkey." I stopped binging and vomiting entirely. I had doctors and my family to help me.

My body was like an infant's, being introduced to food for the first time. It had to be "trained" to accept food again, in very small amounts at first so it could be kept down. I had to learn to eat all over again. Gradually, I began to bring my eating under control. Thoughts of binging and vomiting entered my mind, but eventually the time came when the thoughts left me.

I was truly changing inside and liking myself. Food was no longer my world. My relationship with my family was improving, I was making friends and working and concentrating on living my life. I moved into an apartment with my sister. I was becoming stronger every day.

Within five months I gained over twenty-five pounds. For the first time in my life I saw myself with weight on my frame. And I no longer had a child's body—I had a bust and a few curves. I kept asking everyone how I looked, because I wasn't sure. I am sure now. I am very pleased with how I look. I no longer look like an "it." I look like the young woman I am.

The desperation and hopelessness I once felt have left me. I realize how important I am to me and to the people who care about me. And I am now able to care about and give support to others who are suffering. I can share myself with others because I am no longer afraid of sliding backwards. Life may seem hard at times, but it is precious to me—and truly worth living.

A Few Words in Closing...

You have seen that anorexia nervosa and bulimia nervosa can be frightening, painful, and dangerous disorders. But you have also seen that anorexics and bulimics *can* recover. When the warning signs are heeded and treatment is sought, the outlook is encouraging.

Unfortunately, the total number of cases of anorexia and bulimia seems to be rising. As long as our culture puts such great emphasis upon thinness and dieting, we can probably expect this trend to persist.

Of course, we have also stressed that anorexia and bulimia involve more than just dieting. When a person tries so hard to control calories, she or he is probably longing to control something far more crucial in life. Eating disorders involve both physical and emotional hunger.

More people are gaining knowledge about these problems, but there is still a great need for public awareness. Try to share your knowledge with others. And if you want to learn more, there are many sources you can consult.

FOR FURTHER INFORMATION...

Books

Andersen, A. *Practical Comprehensive Treatment of Anorexia Nervosa and Bulimia*. John Hopkins University Press, 1985.

Aronson, V. *A Practical Guide to Optimal Nutrition*. John Wright Publishing, Inc., 1982.

Boskind-White, M. and White, W. C., Jr. *Bulimarexia: The Binge-Purge Cycle*. W.W. Norton and Company, Inc., 1983.

Bruch, H. *Eating Disorders: Obesity, Anorexia Nervosa, and the Person Within*. Basic Books, 1979.

Bruch, H. *The Golden Cage: The Enigma of Anorexia Nervosa*. Harvard University Press, 1978.

Cauwels, J. M. *Bulimia: The Binge-Purge Compulsion*. Doubleday and Company, 1983.

Chernin, K. *The Obsession*. Harper and Row, 1982.

Crisp, A. H. *Anorexia Nervosa: Let Me Be*. Grune & Stratton, 1982.

Darby, P. L., et al. *Anorexia Nervosa: Recent Developments in Research*. Alan R. Liss, Inc., 1983.

Garfinkel, P. E., and Garner, D. W. *Anorexia Nervosa: A Multidimensional Perspective*. Brunner/Mazel, Inc., 1982.

Garfinkel, P. E., and Garner, D. W. *Handbook of Psychotherapy for Anorexia Nervosa and Bulimia*. Guilford Press, 1985.

Gross, M. *Anorexia Nervosa: A Comprehensive Approach*. The Collamore Press, 1982.

Hall, L., and Cohn, L. *Understanding and Overcoming*

Bulimia: A Self-Help Guide. Gurze Books, 1982.

Havekamp, K. *The Empty Face.* Richard Marek, Publisher, 1978.

Hudlow, E. E. *Alabaster Chambers.* St. Martin's Press, Inc., 1979.

Hutchinson, M. G. *Transforming Body Image: Learning to Love the Body You Have.* The Crossing Press, 1985.

Josephs, R. *Early Disorder.* Farrar, Strauss, and Giroux, 1980.

Kano, S. *Making Peace with Food: A Step-by-Step Guide to Freedom from Diet-Weight Conflict.* Amity Publishing Company, 1985.

Kinoy, B. P., and Miller, E. B., eds. *When Will We Laugh Again? Living and Dealing with Anorexia Nervosa and Bulimia.* Columbia University Press, 1984.

Latimer, J. R. *Reflections on Recovery: Freedom from Bulimia and Compulsive Overeating.* Mesa Productions, 1984.

Levenkron, S. *Kessa.* Warner Books, 1986.

Levenkron, S. *The Best Little Girl in the World.* Contemporary Books, Inc., 1979.

Levenkron, S. *Treating and Overcoming Anorexia Nervosa.* Charles Scribner's Sons, 1982.

Liu, A. *Solitaire.* Harper and Row, 1979.

MacLeod, S. *The Art of Starvation: A Story of Anorexia and Survival.* Schocken Books, 1982.

Minuchin, S., et al. *Psychosomatic Families: Anorexia Nervosa in Context.* Harvard University Press, 1978.

O'Neill, C. B. *Starving for Attention.* Continuum Publishing Company, 1982.

Orbach, S. *Fat Is a Feminist Issue.* Berkeley Books, 1978.

Palazzoli, M. S. *Self Starvation.* Jason Aronson, Inc., 1985.

Pope, H. G., Jr., and Hudson, J. *New Hope for Binge Eaters: Advances in the Understanding and Treatment of Bulimia.* Harper and Row, 1985.

Roth, G. *Feeding the Hungry Heart: The Experience of Compulsive Eating.* New American Library, 1983.

Ruckman, I. *The Hunger Scream.* Walker & Company, Inc., 1983.

Sours, J. A. *Starving to Death in a Sea of Objects.* Jason Aronson, Inc., 1980.

Squire, S. *The Slender Balance: Causes and Cures for Bulimia, Anorexia, and the Weight-Loss/Weight-Gain Seesaw.* Putnam, 1983.

Vincent, L. M. *Competing with the Sylph.* Andrews and McMeel, Inc., 1979.

Vredevelt, P., and Whitman, J. *Walking a Thin Line: Anorexia and Bulimia, the Battle Can Be Won.* Multnomah Press, 1985.

Lesson Plan

The Psychology of Eating Disorders: A Lesson Plan for Grades 7-12. Written by Michael Levine, Ph.D., of Kenyon College. Available through the National Anorexic Aid Society, 5796 Karl Road, Columbus, Ohio 43229, (614) 436-1112. (Five fifty-minute sessions including materials for visual aids, role plays, and handouts.)

Professional Journal

Strober, M., ed. *The International Journal of Eating Disorders.* Bimonthly, John Wiley and Sons, Inc.

Newsletter

NAAS Quarterly Newsletter, 5796 Karl Road, Columbus, Ohio 43229. Material is appropriate for professional and personal use. Ten back issues and "Overview of Eating Disorders" can be ordered for $10. Current subscription available through NAAS memberships.

~*~

Audio-Visual Materials

Dieting—The Danger Point. McGraw-Hill Films, 674 Via de la Valle, P.O. Box 641, Del Mar, CA 92014 (20 minutes, 16-mm or videocassette, teacher's guide).

The Hunger Artist: A Portrait of Anorexia Nervosa. Fat Chance Films, 390 Elizabeth Street, San Francisco, CA 94114, (415) 925-2678 (30 minutes, 16-mm color documentary).
Donations to: The Independent Documentary Group
394 Elizabeth Street
San Francisco, CA 94114

I Don't Have to Hide: A Film About Anorexia and Bulimia. Fanlight Productions, 47 Halifax Street, Jamaica Plain, MA 02130, (617) 524-0980 (28 minutes, 16-mm, color).

Killing Us Softly. Cambridge Documentary Films, Inc., P.O. Box 385, Cambridge, MA 02139, (617) 354-3677 (30 minutes, 16-mm film).

Measure of Worth. Women Make Movies, Inc., 225 Lafayette, Room 212, New York, NY 10012, (212) 925-0606 (15 minutes, black and white, 16-mm documentary).

Wasting Away: Understanding Anorexia Nervosa and Bulimia. Guidance Associates, Inc., Communications Park, Box 3000, Mount Kisco, NY 10549-9989, 1-800-431-1242 (from New York state, Alaska, or Hawaii, call collect [914] 666-4100) (30 minutes, on Beta, VHS, or ¾-inch U-Matic).

NATIONAL SELF-HELP AND SUPPORT GROUPS

AABA–American Anorexic Bulimia Association
133 Cedar Lane
Teaneck, NJ 07666
(201) 836-1800

ABC–Anorexia Bulimia Center, Inc.
P.O. Box 213
Lincoln Center, MA 01773
(617) 259-9767

ANAD–Anorexia Nervosa and Associated Disorders
Box 7
Highland Park, IL 60035
(312) 831-3438

ANRED–Anorexia and Related Disorders
P.O. Box 5102
1255 Hillyard
Eugene, OR 97405
(503) 344-1144

BASH–Bulimia Anorexia Self-Help
6125 Clayton Avenue, Suite 215
St. Louis, MO 63139
(314) 567-4080

Center for the Study of Anorexia and Bulimia
One West 91st Street
New York, NY 10024
(212) 595-3449

NAAS–National Anorexic Aid Society, Inc.
5796 Karl Road
Columbus, OH 43229
(614) 436-1112

Index

63

males and eating disorders, 14
menstruation, 21, 26, 30

NAAS Newsletter, 42
National Anorexic Aid Society, 42
nutritional counseling, 35

one-to-one therapy, 34

physical dangers of eating disorders, 30-31
physical factors in eating disorders, 14, 18-21, 26, 27, 29, 30-31
psychological factors in eating disorders, 14, 19-21, 22-23, 26-27
purging, 21

secrecy, and bulimics, 21-23
self-esteem, 13-15, 21-22, 23, 26-27
self-help organizations, 36
sexuality, 26
"shelter of childhood," 26
stress and eating disorders, 11, 19-20, 22, 25-26, 31
support groups, 34
syndrome, 14

thinness as a goal, 19, 20, 22, 23, 26; cultural emphasis on, 27-29
Tilton, Patricia Howe, 41-46

vomiting, 19, 21, 23; dangers of, 30-31

warning signs, of anorexia nervosa, 20-21; of bulimia nervosa, 23
weight and culture, 27-29; control of, 11, 18, 19, 23, 27-29
weight gain, fear of, 20
weight loss, and anorexia, 18-20; and bulimia, 22-23